The Warrior Workbook

A Guide for Conquering Your Worry Monster

Dan Peters, Ph.D.
with Lisa Reid, Ed.D.
and Stephanie Davis, M.Ed.

Gifted Unlimited, LLC
www.giftedunlimitedllc.com

The Warrior Workbook: A Guide for Conquering Your Worry Monster
Cover design: Hutchison-Frey
Interior design: The Printed Page
Edited by: Asa Bush and Kama Cannon

Published by Gifted Unlimited, LLC
12340 US Highway 42 #453
Goshen, KY 40026

17 16 15 14 13   5 4 3 2 1

Library of Congress Cataloging-in-Publication Data

Names: Peters, Daniel B., 1970- author. | Reid, Lisa, 1975- author. | Davis,

   Stephanie, 1965- author.
Title: From worrier to warrior : a workbook and journal / Daniel B. Peters,
   Ph.D., Lisa Reid, Ed.D., Stephanie Davis, M.Ed.
Description: Tucson, AZ : Great Potential Press, Inc., [2016]
Identifiers: LCCN 2016042137 | ISBN 9781935067443 (pbk.)
Subjects: LCSH: Worry in children--Problems, exercises, etc.--Juvenile
   literature. | Anxiety in children--Problems, exercises, etc.--Juvenile
   literature. | Fear in children--Problems, exercises, etc.--Juvenile
   literature.
Classification: LCC BF723.W67 P4683 2016 | DDC 155.4/1246--dc23 LC record
available at https://lccn.loc.gov/2016042137

ISBN 10: 1-935067-44-3
ISBN 13: 978-1-935067-44-3

Dedication

To Peter Holt

Thank you for caring so much,
and for all that you have made possible in the lives of students,
teachers, and families. With great respect, care, and gratitude.

Acknowledgments

A huge thank you to the students who lent their voices, expertise and time, into putting this journal together. Sitting on the classroom rug, they edited and revised what they felt were the most helpful strategies out of *From Worrier to Warrior*. Their courage and openness is an inspiration to all of us and everyone using this workbook.

We would also like to acknowledge Jim Webb, Janet Gore, and the wonderful Great Potential Press team. This workbook is in our hands because they continue to be passionate about, and believe in, helping people of all ages live fully and maximize their potential. This meaningful project was due to their collaborative approach and gentle guidance.

Dan's personal acknowledgement

Thank you, Stephanie, for persevering with the idea that there needed to be a Worry Monster workbook. It was needed, and now we have it! Thank you, Lisa, for taking the initial workbook draft, and improving the important elements of the book by integrating new and interesting activities and information. I value our collaboration and your commitment to your students.

Lisa's personal acknowledgement

Thank you, Dr. Dan Peters, for believing in me and in our mission as a school program. You dedicated so much time, work, guidance, and heart toward our efforts and you invited our community to participate in the creation of this journal.

Many thanks to Beth Ruekberg, Debbie Fischer Oleisky, and the educators at Garrison Forest School who showed me, first hand, the difference that caring, enthusiastic teachers can make in the learning and life experience of a child.

Thank you, Carl Sabatino and Marti Colglazier from Bridges Academy, for all that I have learned from you; you cared about and supported my development as an educator, and your leadership was inspiring.

Thank you, Dr. Ann Kaganoff, Marcy Dann, and all of the members of the Association of Educational Therapists in Orange County, for your invaluable mentorship and advocacy of Reid Day School.

Stephanie's personal acknowledgement

I would like to thank Dr. Dan Peters for welcoming my thoughts and for allowing me to collaborate on this journal. All your books and this journal are life-changing for people of all ages who suffer from worry/anxiety.

Thank you to my son, Cole, and his personal Worry Monster, who taught me the importance of recording a problem/worry, the size of it, and the outcomes (usually good). This trail of positive evidence immediately minimizes the Worry Monster!

Thank you to Danielle Smith for inviting me into your classroom, to teach me the best practices for calming the mind and body with an innovative and multi-sensory approach.

Table of Contents

Introduction

A few years ago, I wrote **Make Your Worrier a Warrior** and **From Worrier to Warrior**. Since then, countless numbers of children, teens, and adults have "taken down" the Worry Monster by using the strategies they learned in these books; they now live with courage and are able to cope with life's expected and unexpected challenges. Everywhere I went, people asked me, "Is there a workbook to defeat the Worry Monster?"

The answer now is YES! You are holding this workbook because two awesome educators (Lisa and Stephanie) and four awesome kids (Cole, Grayson, Myles, and Scarlett) were determined to make the Worry Monster books into a workbook because they wanted to help all kids have the courage to take down the Worry Monster. They wanted you to know that you are not alone, that you are strong and courageous, and that you CAN live with less worry and fear.

I continue to admire the people I see every day who stand up to the Worry Monster and drive that troublemaker away so they can enjoy their lives and have the courage to reach their potential and pursue their passions. Each of you has so much to offer the world, and we cannot let the Worry Monster keep you from meeting your personal goals and following your dreams.

I KNOW you can take the Worry Monster down and stand with courage as you discover all that you can be—just like Cole, Grayson, Myles, Scarlett, Lisa, Stephanie, and me.

Welcome to your Warrior training. Welcome to our team. Let's do this!

~ Dr. Dan

Dear _____,

Because I believe in you and know that you can be an amazing warrior, I am giving you this book. You may have been worried lately, and your worries may even have felt scary at times. But as you work through the activities in this book, you will realize that you can make your worries smaller. You can even make them go away. It will take effort and courage, but I know you can do it. You can manage, control, and even defeat the Worry Monster.

Everyone experiences the Worry Monster in one way or another, so always remember that you are not alone in your feelings. There will always be others around to help you and who understand that your feelings matter. Things do get better. They did for the other worriers who used this journal and workbook, and they will for you, too!

Sincerely,

"Sometimes the smallest step in the right direction
ends up being the biggest step of your life.
Tiptoe if you must, but take a step."
~ Naeem Callaway

The Worry Box

One of the first things you can do to help you overcome your worries, is to recognize them and start to give yourself a break from thinking about them. Often, worries may actually sort themselves out if we set them aside for a while.

Feeling worried? If so, just write down your worry and put it in a Worry Box. It will be nice and safe there, so you can leave it without fear. It's like putting the Worry Monster in a cage. When it's time to visit and work on making a worry go away for good, you can always take it out and talk to it. For now, just save it for your worry time, when it will be easier to figure out and manage. You can always put it back in the Worry Box again. Over time, you may find you don't miss it, and that what seemed like a big worry before is no longer a worry at all!

This is a Worry Ticket. When you have a worry, cut out a Worry Ticket, write your thoughts on the back, and place it for safekeeping in your Worry Box.

Some Worry Tickets for you to use are in the back of this journal on page 92. You can make a copy of that page and cut out the Worry Tickets so you will have as many as you need, or you can make them up yourself.

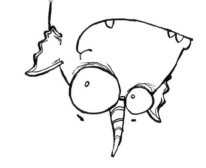

CHAPTER 1

It's Easy to Worry about a Lot of Things!

"Worry is a useless mulling over of things we cannot change."
~ Peace Pilgrim

"You don't have to control your thoughts.
You just have to stop letting them control you."
~ Dan Millman

"I learned that courage was not the absence of fear,
but the triumph over it. The brave man is not he who
does not feel afraid, but he who conquers that fear."
~ Nelson Mandela

You Are Not the Only One: Examples of Worriers

Before we learn about who the Worry Monster is, take a moment to read about a few young people who have also been challenged by worries and worrying. You might you have some things in common.

Sierra

Sierra is 6 years old and in 1st grade. She is afraid to be alone, so she follows her mother around the house and needs her to come with her into to her bedroom, and even into the bathroom. She calls to her mother when she wakes up—at all hours of the night—to come be with her. Drop-off at school is tough because Sierra wants to cling to her mother and doesn't want to let her go. Sierra's mom has to stay with her at birthday parties and after-school activities or else Sierra will refuse to participate in them.

Ben

Ben is 9 years old and a 3rd grader. He worries about bad things happening, though he is not sure exactly what the bad things are. He is always asking his mother and his teacher to reassure him that things will be okay—for example, that he is doing his schoolwork the way he is supposed to. Ben worries he will get in trouble at school, and that his classmates may, too. He bites his fingernails and chews on his shirt, but isn't aware he is doing so. He often complains of having a stomachache.

Phil

Phil is 10 and in 4th grade. He always seems to be worrying about something that could happen. He works hard to do well in school and wants to please his parents and teachers. Most people don't know how much he worries because he keeps it to himself. He tells himself that he will stop worrying once he completes a project or after playing well in an important soccer game, but there always seems to be something new to worry about.

Jenny

Jenny, who is 11 years old, has just begun the 6th grade at a new middle school, but her best friends from elementary all now attend a different middle school. Her teachers say she daydreams a lot and seems to be in a daze during class. Jenny says that she feels sick at school, and worries about throwing up. Because of this, she often begs to stay home from school. When she does stay home, however, she seems fine. She also seems to be normal or "herself" on weekends.

Casey

Casey is 12, and she feels like she has to touch things a certain way to feel okay. If she touches one of her legs, she feels like she has to touch the other leg in the same way so that they are balanced. When she walks into her room, she has to touch her door five times or else she feels funny and uptight. She counts numbers in her head while she's walking to school, and if she loses track of the numbers, she has to go back to the last place she remembered them and start all over again. She says that if she doesn't do these things, something bad might happen.

Mateo

Mateo is 11 years old, in the 5th grade, and has always struggled with social situations. He has trouble looking people in the eye when he talks to them. When he speaks, he fears he will have nothing interesting to say, or will say something stupid and be laughed at. Mateo feels like everyone else does things better than he does, and that he will never achieve his goals in life. When things don't turn out as he had hoped, he becomes upset and overwhelmed, saying things like, "What if I can't take care of myself when I grow up?" or "What if I never have a really deep, meaningful friendship?" His parents say he seems to carry the weight of the world on his shoulders. After school and on weekends, he stays home playing video games and cannot be encouraged to call kids he knows from school to make plans with them. He doesn't want to join activities at his school because he's convinced he will be no good at them and that his classmates won't like him.

Sophie

Sophie, age 12 and in 6th grade, has always been a high achiever. In school, her grades are almost always As and A+s. She is so busy and takes such hard classes that she stays up late studying because feels she needs to do her work perfectly. She also plays several sports, and she volunteers in the community. Yet, even though her work is excellent, she is rarely proud of her accomplishments. To her, life is "a grind." She often feels tense and stressed, and she worries about what will happen if she doesn't get into a top college.

The worries and fears of the children and teenagers we describe here are not unique. Many young people everywhere feel the same way. Do any of the people in these stories worry about the same things you do? Can you relate to any of their stories? If so, circle the name or names of the young people you relate to:

Sierra   **Ben**   **Phil**   **Sophie**

Jenny   **Casey**   **Mateo**

Next, write out what sounded familiar to you on the lines that follow.

For example:

"I related to Ben's story because I feel that people don't know how much I worry... because I keep it to myself."

_____

_____

_____

_____

_____

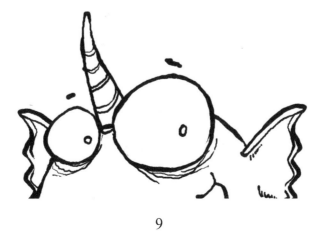

Introducing the Worry Monster

All of these worries come from the Worry Monster. Let me introduce you to that troublemaker—a ridiculous guy who makes you feel worried and scared—and we are going to show the Worry Monster who is boss!

Take the first step in taming the Worry Monster.

Color the Worry Monster in any way you want to show that pest how silly this mischief-maker is.

Things to Remember

☺ The Worry Monster acts like a bully by making us feel like we're not in control of our thoughts and feelings.

☺ The Worry Monster tricks us into feeling scared and worried.

☺ You will learn to drive the Worry Monster away so that you can be less worried and scared.

CHAPTER 2
Anxiety and Fear

"Our fatigue is often caused not by work, but by worry,
frustration, and resentment."

~ Dale Carnegie

"I've lived through some terrible things in my life,
some of which actually happened."

~ Mark Twain

There are some important words for you to know to help you conquer the Worry Monster.

Important Word #1

Irrational: Another word for unreasonable—and probably not true.

"There are two kinds of fears:
rational and irrational—or in simpler terms,
fears that make sense and fears that don't."
~ Daniel Handler

Anxiety is an irrational fear, and the Worry Monster tricks us into having uncomfortable and scary feelings by messing with our thoughts. He makes us think there is a BIG chance of something bad happening when, in fact, the chance is VERY small—and that's irrational. And even if it did happen, just how awful would it really be? Would civilization stop? Would everyone truly hate you? Would your life truly be over?

Can you think of an example of an irrational fear that you have, or used to have? Or, maybe a fear someone else had that was irrational? Can you describe it?

_____

Why do you think that fear is irrational? Do you have any proof that it is irrational? List it here:

_____

Everyone experiences the Worry Monster at least occasionally, but in different ways—just as we all have irrational thoughts about different things.

"One time, I was at the beach with my family. I looked out at the ocean and it stretched so far that it looked like it curved up and I thought it was a Tsunami. Even though I know now that it wasn't a Tsunami, I still worry every time I go to the beach."

~ *Grayson*

Important Word #2

Amygdala: A very small, almond-shaped part of the brain that is involved in emotion, particularly anger and fear.

Pronounced: *uh-MIG-duh-luh*

"The amygdala in the emotional center sees and hears everything that occurs to us instantaneously and is the trigger point for the fight or flight response.
~ Daniel Goleman

Our body acts in strange ways when we are worried or scared, and a few small parts of our brain is where it starts. One of these is the amygdala, which is a very small, almond-shaped group of cells (called neurons), and the amygdala is the emotional center of our bodies. The amygdala is located in the "primitive" part of our brain, and it controls the "fight or flight" response the body uses to deal with fear. The amygdala controls the body's automatic response to fight or run away from something it sees as a threat, and it is part of the brain called the limbic system, which not only deals with emotion, but also with memories around that emotion.

FUN FACT: Did you know goose bumps exist to help animals survive in the wild? They cause your hair (and other animal's hair) to stick up in order to trap a layer of heat close to the body to keep it warm in the cold, AND when the hair stands up (called our pilomotor reflex) because of fear, it makes the animal look larger and more scary.

Wow! The Worry Monster can even bother the hair on your arms!

You probably already know that the different parts of your brain talk to each other, but did you know that the amygdala can sometimes mix up the whole message!?

The amygdala can be very irrational. That "nutty" almond shape can make you think and feel like you need to worry, even when you don't need to! Fortunately, though, there is another part of the brain that helps deal with the amygdala when it acts irrationally. It's called the Prefrontal Cortex in the Frontal Lobe.

Your Prefrontal Cortex helps you think so you can make good decisions. When your Amygdala charges forward with a fight or flight response, your Prefrontal Cortex immediately begins to work trying to convince the amygdala (and its fight or flight response) to calm down so it can think things through.

Sometimes, though, the Amygdala overpowers and hijacks the Prefrontal Cortex, and then the Amygdala brings into the action another part of the brain—the Hippocampus, which helps you store information into your long-term memory. This long-term storage can be very helpful when there really is something you need to remember to be careful about. But when your Amygdala tells your Hippocampus to store an irrational fear, your memory keeps it for a long time and may trick you into thinking that you need to keep responding that way—every time, even when it is an irrational fear. Your brain can actually fool your body into thinking it needs to worry, just by feeling worried!

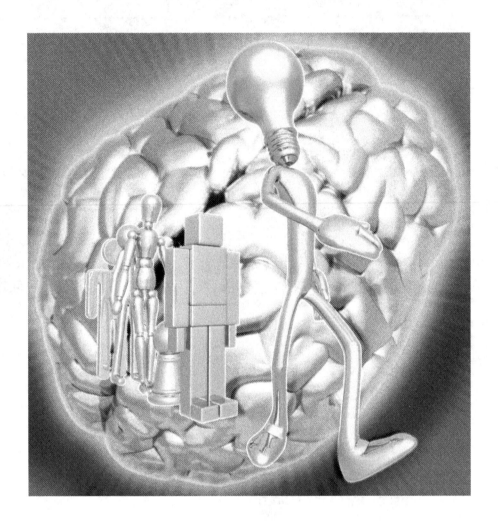

Your Beautiful Brain!

☺ Color your Frontal Lobe blue

☺ Color your Hippocampus green

☺ Color your Amygdala red

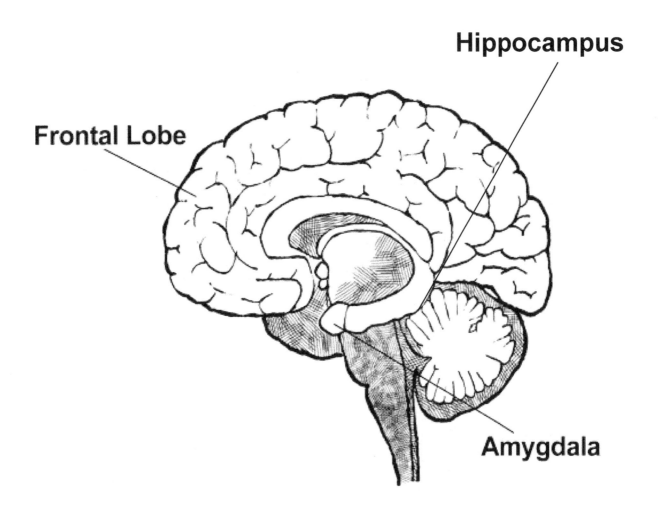

Frontal Lobe

Hippocampus

Amygdala

Beyond the Brain

The brain is not the only part that gets caught up in the action. Your brain also sends messages to the rest of the body.

When your amygdala tells your brain "fight or flight," it also sends messages to another part of your body called the adrenal gland.

The adrenal gland produces adrenaline, a chemical made by the body that increases your heart and breathing rate. Adrenaline moves blood from your stomach and brain into your muscles, making you stronger— at least temporarily! Adrenaline is helpful if you are faced with a real threat, but if you have an irrational fear, it can trick you into thinking that a danger is real by making it seem realistic and convincing. In this situation, your adrenaline is feeding the Worry Monster.

FUN FACT: The world record for heavy lifting is 1,003 pounds. But there have been rare instances, outside of athletic competition, of something called Hysterical (or Superhuman) Strength. Hysterical Strength gives people the (temporary) ability to lift much more than they otherwise could. This flood of strength is caused by an adrenaline surge and is responsible for several heroic incidents; people have been known to lift as much as 3,000 pounds in emergency situations. That's like lifting a car! One mother even fought a 700-pound polar bear in defense of her 7-year-old son!

The amygdala, which gives us our "survival" response to feelings of fear, causes our body to feel a certain way in stressful situations. Here are the parts of the body affected by changes in the amygdala. Hopefully, this will help you understand why your body acts the way it does when you are scared:

☺ *Heart and Lungs:* When you are scared, your heart beats faster; your chest gets tight; and sometimes you breathe faster and feel like you can't get enough air. Your body speeds up your heart and lungs in order to send more blood into your muscles so they are stronger. This occurs so that you can fight and run better.

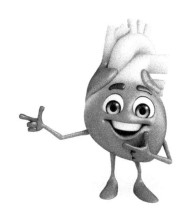

☺ *Stomach:* Stomach pain is another way fear can affect the body; fear can cause nausea, and even sometimes diarrhea. This happens because much of the blood leaves your stomach and intestines and pumps into your heart, lungs, and muscles—in case you need to run away or fight. Remember, your amygdala is part of the "old brain", and it is more concerned with your ability to escape saber-tooth tigers than with whether or not you digest your macaroni and cheese.

☺ *Brain:* Being scared can make you feel dizzy, light-headed, or cause other strange feelings. It can make you feel like you're about to faint, or that you're losing control, or even like you're going crazy. This is because, when you're scared, your blood has to leave your brain in order to get into your heart, lungs, and muscles.

☺ ***Arms and Legs:*** Fear can cause you to start sweating, shaking, trembling. You can get cold hands, numbness, muscle tenseness, and even feel pain. The reason this happens is, when you're scared, your blood leaves your skim—so you won't bleed as much if you get hurt. Isn't that cool? We are designed so well for survival that the blood even leaves our skin so we can do better in battle!

Use what you have learned to describe what reactions the different parts of a person's body might have when they are scared.

Brain_____

_____

Heart and Lungs_____

_____

Stomach_____

_____

Arms and Legs_____

_____

The Worry Monster may use different parts of your body and brain to try and trick you. Remember, each of us has our own reaction to anxiety, and our bodies can feel very differently. Circle the place in your body where **you** feel the Worry Monster when he creeps in and makes you feel scared.

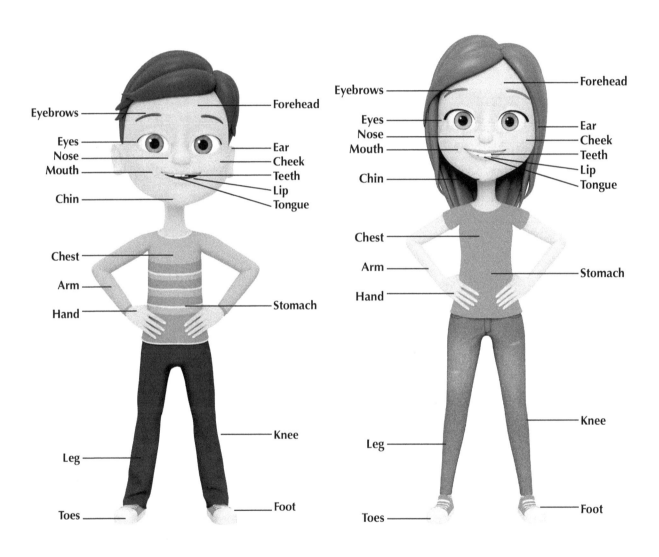

Remember, each of us has our own reaction to anxiety, and our bodies can feel very differently. Scarlett, for example explained the way the Worry Monster makes her feel like this:

"My brain feels hot when I am scared. I
feel annoyed and frustrated and my heart
beats a little bit faster. I feel nauseous,
and when I am really afraid, my arms and legs
feel so heavy that it is hard to walk."

– Scarlett

Where do you feel the Worry Monster when he creeps in and makes you feel scared? Describe how your body feels when you are afraid.

_____

_____

_____

_____

The great news is that those scary feelings ALWAYS go away eventually. They may feel like they won't, but they do, just like an itch. Just hang on. "Ride the wave," and know that it will be over soon!

Things to Remember:

Test your knowledge by filling in the blanks below!

☺ The _____'s job is to sense danger and trigger our survival or "fight or flight" response.

☺ Large amounts of _____ are activated to make us into super-human fighting or running machines.

☺ This _____ makes our body—brain, stomach, heart, lungs, arms, and legs—feel a certain way.

☺ We all get some type of "whoosh" feelings that let us know when the Worry Monster is _____.

☺ We need to turn on our thinking brain in order to turn down our _____ brain.

☺ The more we realize and talk about the Worry Monster's tricks, the _____ he gets.

Word Bank

weaker   amygdala   survive

adrenaline   visiting   emotional

You don't have to let the Worry Monster control you!

As you learn about the amygdala and the other parts of your brain, you can learn to sense when the amygdala is "kicking in." And once you know this, you'll be able to check yourself, talk to yourself—and undo the Worry Monster's tricks.

At first, it can be hard to know if the Worry Monster is messing with you, but that's okay! With practice, you can learn the Worry Monster's tricks. Remember, if you're not sure whether a worry or concern is real, or whether it's irrational, you can always check with a parent, teacher, or another trusted adult. Your feelings are real, and they are important.

List the people you can go to when your amygdala is "kicking in," and who will help you to "ride the wave" until the worry is gone.

1._____

2._____

3._____

CHAPTER 3

Types of Anxiety and What They Look Like

"Worry does not empty tomorrow of its sorrow.
It empties today of its strength."

~ Corrie Ten Boon

"It's sad, actually, because my anxiety keeps me from enjoying
things as much as I should at this age."

~ Amanda Seyfried

Worries and fears are also called **anxieties**. And the Worry Monster uses many different kinds of anxieties to make people feel bad. But there is something you can do!

The first step in getting the Worry Monster to back off is identifying and labeling the different anxieties you might be feeling. Giving a name to something is often the first step to overcoming it.

Here are some descriptions of different types of anxiety:

General Anxiety

General anxiety is basically just another way of talking about the Worry Monster. It describes what happens when a person experiences ongoing worry—a kind of worry that affects a person more than is necessary. This type of worry seems to be there constantly, and that worry finds its way into almost any situation or thought ("When will you be home?" "What if something bad happens?" "Do I look okay?" "What if I make a mistake?" "What if I don't get picked?"). People who experience general anxiety are nearly always worried! They worry about almost everything.

Anxiety Attacks

An anxiety attack is the sensation of intense physical feelings related to the sudden flow of adrenaline to the body. Anxiety attacks are sometimes so severe they become a panic attack, where feelings of worry or fear make you so scared you think you might pass out. And even though an anxiety attack is not as bad as a full-blown panic attack, it still feels awful! A lot of kids have anxiety attacks when they're in situations that frighten them.

Agoraphobia

Agoraphobia refers to a person's irrational fear of their environment. Usually, someone with agoraphobia is afraid the environment will be unpredictable or dangerous in some way. The person worries that if they are in a strange environment, they might have a panic attack (whether they have had one before or not), which would be embarrassing, particularly if they can't escape the situation. So people with agoraphobia seek to avoid certain environments at all costs. Because the person wants to avoid the panic attack, which might be embarrassing, he avoids the place or situation where he fears he might experience an attack. In this way, agoraphobia may be thought of as a person's fear of fear.

Agoraphobia prevents a person from going out to enjoy even ordinary activities. Let's say, for example, that Joey has a panic attack in a large supermarket and then becomes afraid it is going to happen again. As a result, Joey refuses to go to any supermarket. Next, he gets the same bodily sensations and fears when his family is in a restaurant, because the food smells similar to a supermarket, so he decides he is not going to any more restaurants. He then starts to fear a variety of other buildings. Before long, Joey is approaching full-blown agoraphobia, and refuses to leave his house to go anywhere! His fear of the Worry Monster keeps him from doing anything.

Obsessive-Compulsive Disorder (OCD)

OCD is a type of anxiety that causes people to have repetitive thoughts or ideas. Sometimes these ideas are scary, or embarrassing, but they are always tough to make go away. People who have these kinds of repetitive thoughts often also feel a compulsion to go with them; they feel compelled to do something (such as tapping, or counting, or doing things a "certain way") over and over again, as this relieves the anxiety or worry produced by their scary or embarrassing thought. Most people think of OCD in terms of flipping light switches on and off repeatedly or washing one's hands more than is necessary, and these are common OCD behaviors. But behind these behaviors are irrational Worry Monster thoughts that are very distressing and won't go away. In most cases, the person <u>has</u> to do something to feel okay, like touch the doorway in a certain place when walking through it, tap each one of her legs the same number of times, or kiss both sides of her mom's or dad's face before bedtime. The Worry Monster can make you do some very unusual and strange things to try to control your fears.

Specific Phobia

Phobia is another word for fear. A specific phobia is a fear that is extreme and unreasonable and is brought on by a specific object, like bugs, or planes, or elevators, or by a specific situation, like public speaking. The irrational fear is that something terrible, horrible, or awful might occur. Sometimes phobias are easy to avoid, such as keeping away from insects by never going camping or avoiding planes by never flying. Other phobias are more difficult to avoid, like being afraid of dogs or loud noises, and they can cause significant difficulty for you and your family. When you think about a situation that makes you uncomfortable and then you are able to avoid it, the anxiety goes away; you feel safe. Unfortunately, though, that means the Worry Monster has won—at least for now—because you are going to be even less likely in the future to try to overcome your irrational phobia.

Social Phobia

A social phobia is a constant fear of social situations where you are around unfamiliar people. People who suffer from social phobia are often afraid of being criticized or humiliated if they have to perform or speak in front of a group. Basically, a social phobia is the fear of embarrassment or humiliation. A person with social phobia might think, "Those kids are going to laugh at me." "They're making fun of me." "Look how they're looking at me." "I don't belong here." "What are they going to say?" and even, "What if I look funny?" Kids with social phobia imagine what others might be thinking about them all the time. When this happens, the Worry Monster is able to step in and hijack their thinking.

Now, there could be some truth to these statements, right? We all get these feelings from time to time, but what we're talking about when we refer to social anxiety is whether the response is extreme. An extreme response would be one that interferes with your well-being, or affects your life in a significant way. For example, extreme social phobia behavior may include refusing to participate in school activities or in events like birthday parties and family gatherings, or even refusing to go to school.

Post-Traumatic Stress Disorder (PTSD)

Post-Traumatic Stress Disorder, known as PTSD, is a common problem for our soldiers who have returned from war where they experienced trauma from seriously scary situations like being in gunfights or were injured by bombs. But PTSD can also apply to anyone who experiences other kinds of trauma—perhaps a near-death experience, or someone else's near-death experience, or any situation where there is intense fear. This could include being in a tornado or a car accident or even seeing a bad accident. A person could also have PTSD after seeing a serious fight or being in a home where the family members have terrible fights. The Worry Monster can have a great time here because there really has been something to worry about in the past. A person with PTSD may feel emotionally numb, experience nightmares, or have flashbacks of the bad experience. The person usually tries to avoid situations that remind him of the earlier traumatic event; he may be jumpy and nervous, or he may have extreme emotional meltdowns.

Separation Anxiety

Separation anxiety happens when a child is afraid to leave her parents and worries that something bad is going to happen to her or her parents while the two of them are apart. Kids who have separation anxiety may feel they really **need** to sleep in their parents' bed, or that they **need** their parents to stay with them at school or at other activities. Kids with separation anxiety feel afraid any time their parents are away.

Perfectionism

Perfectionism is another common way for the Worry Monster to interfere with our lives. The main element of perfectionism is a fear of failure. Some experts think there is a good kind of perfectionism and bad kind of perfectionism. An example of good or healthy perfectionism is trying to be our best, like paying attention to details and working hard to make the best project we can, but not stressing out too much if it's not truly perfect. Bad or unhealthy perfectionism is the kind that makes us feel afraid that we can never be good enough, and where we worry so much that we are miserable.

Eating Disorders

Individuals who are perfectionistic and high-achieving seem to be more likely to have eating disorders. Eating disorders come in many different forms: some where people don't eat enough, some where they eat too much, and even some where they eat and then make themselves vomit. Eating disorders are not often talked about when people talk about anxiety. However, they are anxiety disorders too, and they can become dangerous and even life-threatening if they aren't treated. This is more than someone just being a picky eater. People with eating disorders can actually starve themselves because they don't like the way they look. Eating disorders all involve an obsessive or intense need to have one's body look a certain way—generally more "perfect." This fear, brought on by the Worry Monster, changes the way a person thinks about how they look. It changes the way they see themselves in the mirror, and the way they think about food and eating (and yes, eating disorders affect boys, too).

As you can see, there's a lot of worry to go around! But remember: if any of these responses to worries and fears sound familiar, it doesn't mean there is something wrong with you. It just means you have a Worry Monster following you around and bullying and tricking you into doing things that don't let you live as happily and contentedly as you could be. It is important to learn ways to tame the Worry Monster, and there is something we can do about that!

The first step in getting the Worry Monster to back off is to identify the types of worries and fears you are feeling. Did any of the descriptions sound familiar to you?

Circle any anxieties listed below that seem to apply to you:

Generalized Anxiety

Social Phobia

Panic Attacks

Post-Traumatic Stress Disorder

Anxiety Attacks

Separation Anxiety

Agoraphobia

Perfectionism

Obsessive-Compulsive Disorder

Eating Disorders

Specific Phobia

Sometimes people who feel worried and afraid aren't sure how to describe their feelings; they may not even realize they are feeling anxious. Here is a helpful checklist of some things that people sometimes feel and do when they feel anxious. Put an X next to any that you relate to. Just taking note of these things is helpful because it gives you a "heads up!" that the Worry Monster probably is at work.

- ❑ Headaches
- ❑ Stomachaches
- ❑ Trouble relaxing
- ❑ Low energy
- ❑ Trouble sleeping
- ❑ Feeling like you have to go to the bathroom all of the time
- ❑ Loss of appetite
- ❑ Nail biting
- ❑ Picking at skin
- ❑ Sucking on t-shirts
- ❑ Eating non-food items
- ❑ Being clingy
- ❑ Not going to the bathroom when you need to
- ❑ Needing excessive reassurance that things are okay
- ❑ Worrying that others are talking about you or criticizing you
- ❑ Crying
- ❑ Asking lots of questions
- ❑ Running away
- ❑ Yelling

List others here:

_____

_____

_____

_____

_____

Avoidance: The Worry Monster's Best Friend

If you're feeling worried or afraid of something, it's natural to want to avoid it. You are not alone!

The problem with avoidance is it only makes worry and anxiety stronger. Avoiding a problem may make you feel better because it reduces your fear for a very little while, but it feeds and encourages the Worry Monster. When you avoid a problem, the Worry Monster says, "Well, that worked! I'll just do that to this person again." Make a list of the things you do not like to do and often avoid, delay, or get out of doing.

1. _____

2. _____

3. _____

4. _____

5. _____

Are any of the things on your list due to being scared of what might happen or how you might perform? If so, circle the numbers next to them.

Can you think about a specific time when you avoided doing something you wanted to because you were worried? What would have happened if you hadn't felt like you had to worry that day?

Draw a picture, design, or something else below to represent what that "worry free" situation might have looked like.

Worry Monster Crossword Challenge!

ACROSS

3 This is another word for fear.
5 People with this type of anxiety are very afraid of failure and often feel they are not good enough.
6 This part of the body senses danger and triggers a "fight or flight" response.

DOWN

1 This is another word for a worry or fear.
2 A bully and a trickster who likes to make you feel worried.
4 This makes worry and anxiety stronger.

Answers are on page 93

Important Word #3

Misunderstood: To take words or statements in a wrong way, and failing to understand someone or something correctly.

"Being misunderstood by the people whose opinions you value is absolutely the most painful."

~ Gloria Steinem

When people get the wrong message, they misunderstand you. This may cause you to feel hurt and angry.

Think of our poor friend, the snake. Snakes lash out when they feel threatened, but this gives people the wrong idea about them. In fact, only about 10% of snakes are venomous, and most are harmless unless they are provoked.

Sometimes, when people feel anxious, they "lash out" or act out in other ways. They may even say and do things they do not mean and then feel bad about them afterward. These people's actions can be misunderstood.

When you feel you want to act out or lash out, think about whether your feelings are being caused by a misunderstanding. If other people are misunderstanding you, perhaps you can do something to help them understand what you are really saying or feeling. Also, it is important to remember that any bad feelings will ALWAYS go away. Feelings are just feelings, and you don't need to act on them. Lashing out in anger is never a good idea.

Everyone makes mistakes, and it's okay if you've been frustrated in the past. Understanding your worries and fears, and finding words to help you talk about them will make a big difference!

Remember our friend Grayson? Grayson found it helps him to talk about his mistakes.

"I know that when I lash out at people, they may not want to be my friend. I try not to, but sometimes when I am anxious, I lash out at my little brother."

~ Grayson

CHAPTER 4

Cognitive (Thinking) Model of Anxiety

"When we fill our thoughts with right things,
the wrong ones have no room to enter."

~ Joyce Meyer

"You can't have a better tomorrow
if you are thinking about yesterday all the time."

~ Charles Kettering

"Half our mistakes in life come from feeling
where we ought to think,
and thinking where we ought to feel."

~ John Churton Collins

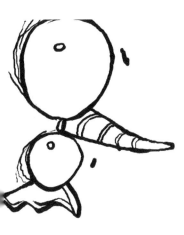

A student told me the following story.

One time, our class went on a field trip, and we had to park in a garage that had several levels. We got out of the car, and everyone started walking toward the elevator. Many of us forgot that one of our classmates is working on her fear of elevators. Instead of getting upset or refusing to go on the trip, she calmly asked, "Can we take the stairs?" and our group happily agreed. The class thought it was actually more fun to go that way!

What can we learn from this story? First, that it's okay to share your worries and to ask for help while you are working to overcome them. It takes courage to express your feelings, and you will find people will respect you for doing so. They will be proud of you for calmly asking for what you need, and doing so will help you overcome your fears more quickly.

What are some things you might be able to say or do instead of lashing out or acting out when you are worried? For example, if you are overwhelmed, you might ask to take a break. Or, if you are not sure how to do something, you can ask for help.

1. _____

2. _____

3. _____

4. _____

5. _____

Thoughts, Feelings, and Behaviors

Our thoughts, behaviors, and feelings are all connected. Changing our thinking can lead to changes in our behaviors and feelings. Similarly, a change in behavior leads to changes in our thinking and feelings. For example, if a student is *feeling* worried about going to a party because he doesn't know who is going to be there, he may find myself *thinking* a worrisome thought like, "I won't have anyone to talk to." He may then get an upset stomach or a headache, and finally decide he wants to *avoid* the party altogether. This student deciding not to go to the party is an example of a *behavior*.

If, on the other hand, the student chooses to *think* about the people from my class who will be there, his stomachache and headache may go away. He will *feel* less worried, and will be more likely to go to the party. So, this student thinking about a different possibility makes him feel less worried, and he goes to the party! This is an example of how thoughts can help change behavior. Make sense?

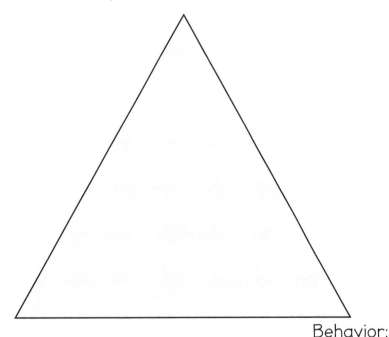

Thought:
"I won't have anyone to talk to at the party!"

Feelings:
"I have a stomach ache."

Behavior:
"Avoid the party."

Can you think of an example of thoughts, feelings, and actions for the Triangle below? You can make one up or think of one that you have experienced.

Thought:

_____

Feelings:

_____

Behavior:

_____

Taking on the Worry Monster

Each time you face the Worry Monster, he gets smaller and less powerful.

...poof!

It takes a lot of courage to face your fears and worries. Make sure to be patient and encourage yourself. You can even give yourself rewards!

How are you going to celebrate your victories over the Worry Monster? Sometimes it helps to think up or brainstorm ideas. In what ways could you reward yourself or celebrate your success? Brainstorm a few ideas for a reward system with your parents or another trusted adult. For example, you might celebrate conquering a fear by going out for frozen yogurt, going for a hike, a little extra play time, or a special dinner. Write your answers in the thought cloud on the next page.

Now that you are starting to get an idea of how the Worry Monster works, it is time to make plans for how to outsmart this troublemaker. What are some things that you think will be better once the Worry Monster has become smaller, or gone away?

1. _____

2. _____

3. _____

"I will be able to go so many more places, and I will feel more confident when my worry is gone!"

~ Scarlett

Chapter 5

Thinking Errors

"You wouldn't worry so much about what others think of you
if you realized how seldom they do."

~ Eleanor Roosevelt

"Nothing is good nor bad but thinking makes it so."

~ Shakespeare

"Positive thinking will let you do everything better
than negative thinking will."

~ Zig Ziglar

The Worry Monster uses our thoughts to make us feel worried and scared. But, as we have recently learned, we can change our feelings by changing our thoughts! In order to do that, we have to know which thoughts are causing the problem, and we need to realize that these thoughts are usually irrational ones.

Have you ever had any of the thoughts listed below? Circle any that sound familiar.

1.   Other people must think I'm stupid.

2.   I never do things right. I always blow it!

3.   I never get picked to be a partner.

4.   I can't make any mistakes!

5.   What will people think if I mess up?

6.   I know the teacher said I did a good job, but she corrected two of my answers, so she really didn't mean it.

7.   I can't go on a field trip without Mom. What if I get lost, and everyone in class leaves without me?

8.   What if burglars break into my house?

9.   They wouldn't let me lead the line walking into the museum, so the whole field trip was ruined.

10. I know Kristie said she liked what I was wearing, but she was laughing with Julie after she looked at me.

11. If I don't get a good grade on this assignment, I'll never get into college.

12. She must have cancelled the party because she didn't want me there.

These irrational thoughts, which some folks call "stinking thinking," almost always stem from one or more thinking errors like these:

☺ All or Nothing—"There is no middle ground or compromise. It will either be magnificent, or it will be horrible."

☺ Catastrophizing—"If it doesn't work out the way I want it to, it will be a catastrophe!"

☺ Mind Reading—"I know what the other person is thinking without even asking them."

☺ Personalizing—"She is making a general statement, but I know that she really is talking about me!"

☺ Overgeneralizing—"Since this was a bad situation before, it will be bad every time it comes up in the future."

☺ Probability Overestimation—"The store elevator is really likely to fall or to trap us inside."

☺ What Will People Think?—"I have to please others all the time. Otherwise, they won't like me."

Remember, you can be a detective with your thoughts! Ask yourself: is what you are thinking really true, or is it a thinking error? What evidence supports your conclusion?

Exercise: Remembering a Time You Beat the Worry Monster!

Some of those negative thoughts might have reminded you of times when you were challenged by the Worry Monster. Can you give an example? Write it below.

_____

_____

What positive qualities or character traits did you use to help you overcome that challenge? Here is a list of examples: adaptable, adventurous, affectionate, agreeable, ambitious, amusing, brave, broad-minded, calm, careful, communicative, compassionate, conscientious, considerate, courteous, creative, decisive, determined, diligent, diplomatic, discreet, easygoing, energetic, enthusiastic, fair-minded, faithful, friendly, generous, gentle, hard-working, helpful, honest, independent, intuitive, inventive, kind, loving, loyal, modest, neat, optimistic, patient, persistent, polite, pro-active, quiet, reliable, resourceful, self-confident, self-disciplined, sincere, sociable, straightforward, sympathetic, thoughtful, tidy, tough, understanding, willing.

_____

_____

Was there someone or something that helped you overcome your worry and fear?

_____

_____

What did you learn from the challenge?

_____

_____

Now try asking a friend or family member these same questions. You'll find that everyone faces the Worry Monster occasionally!

The more you talk to other people about your anxieties and what's bothering you, the more you will realize that you are not alone with your worries.

Examples of worries some kids have told us are listed below:

Are their worries irrational ones? What evidence do you think they have for their worries? What advice would you give to them?

"I worry about tsunamis so much
that I keep glancing at the horizon."
~ Grayson

Evidence: _____

Advice: _____

"Change is scary for me.
I am also afraid of elevators."
~ Scarlett

Evidence: _____

Advice: _____

"I worry about having bad dreams,
and I worry about flunking a test."
~ Myles

Evidence: _____

Advice: _____

"Starting anything new can make me worry."
~ Cole

Evidence:_____

Advice: _____

Everybody worries, and everybody's worries sometimes bother them, just like yours do for you. Listening to others and respecting the way people feel can make a big difference. And if you're worried yourself, remember that you also have a voice. It is a great idea to share your feelings or thoughts with a trusted adult.

The Worry Monster causes lots of problems, but he also helps us to grow and connect with other people. In fact, when you are feeling worried about something, you might want to think about doing something nice for someone else! Doing something nice for someone else helps to calm your amygdala and lowers your sense of worry.

FUN FACT: When you are having a bad day, your body increases the release of a stress hormone called *cortisol*. Cortisol can make random acts of kindness feel like the very last thing that you want to do. But push through that feeling! Going out of your way to do nice things for other people can actually change the way that your body responds to stress. In fact, being kind to others can impact you so much that bad days don't need to mean a bad mood! It sure is hard to feel worried when you are busy being kind.

Think of some things you might be able to do to brighten someone's day. Brainstorm your ideas here.

CHAPTER **6**

Cognitive (Thinking) Strategies

"You don't have to control your thoughts.
You just have to stop letting them control you."
~ *Dan Millman*

"The only person you are destined to be
is the person you decide to be."
~ *Ralph Waldo Emerson*

Time to Take Charge!

Now it is time to use the Worry Monster's own sneaky strategies to defeat him!

You've worked hard to learn about how the Worry Monster works, and now you know that your thoughts determine your feelings and behaviors.

Once you identify your thoughts, feelings, and behaviors, you can begin to chase the Worry Monster away. It may be tough at first, but with patience, practice, and courage you are sure to see great things happen.

There are Four Steps!

1. *Identify the thought*: "What am I thinking about? What is the source of my worry or fear? Is it that I'm scared of taking the test? Or am I scared of what will happen if I happen to fail it?"

2. *Challenge the thought*: "Am I making a thinking error? Is it true that I *always* fail? How likely am I to fail, really? Do I have evidence that says I will fail today? Could this thought be irrational?"

3. *Modify the thought*: "The test is going to be hard, but I am prepared. I usually get nervous before math tests, but generally I do pretty well."

4. *Replace the thought:* "I am prepared. I will try my best and will do fine. If I don't do perfectly, at least I will do good enough. I am choosing not to worry about it, because worrying won't help. Worrying will only feed the Worry Monster."

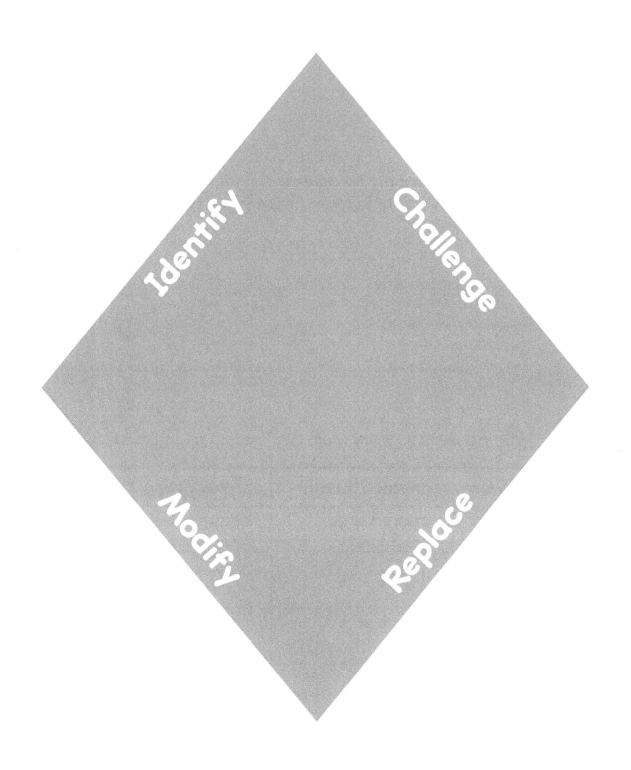

Remember when we talked about the different parts of the brain?

When you use this four-step process, you can stop your irrational brain (run by the amygdala) from running wild. This allows your thinking brain (the frontal lobe) to take over. This will help you think rationally—instead of irrationally—about your worry.

Ready to give it a try? Here's an activity that will help.

Activity:

Think of some Worry Monster thoughts that you may have, as well as some new thoughts you might replace them with. Grayson has a good example:

"Sometimes I think, 'How am I supposed to do this!?' and then I tell myself that I should at least try."

~ Grayson

Now, you write a Worry Monster Thought and then a New Thought.

Worry Monster Thought	My New Thought
"How am I supposed to do this!?"	"I should at least try."

CHAPTER 7

Mindfulness-Based Interventions

"The mind is everything. What you think, you become."

~ Buddha

"The past is already gone; the future is not yet here.
There's only one moment for you to live,
and that is the present moment."

~ Buddha

"Life is ten percent what happens to you,
and ninety percent how you react to it."

~Charles R. Swindell

Staying in the Present: The Single Most Powerful Technique for Keeping the Worry Monster at Bay

One way to practice staying in the present is to learn to rest our minds and bodies. Some people call this meditation and use it to calm themselves down or enter a more peaceful place. Others may call it something else, like visualization. They may use mental exercises to help them stop thinking about their worries, allowing them to open their hearts and minds to new ideas.

What are you doing right now? Would you like to learn one way other Worry Warriors practice staying in the present?

Try this...

☺ Find a comfortable place to sit down.

☺ Sit quietly for 30 seconds. Pay attention to your breathing.

☺ Try and take a few deep calming breaths. Focus on breathing in and out in a slow, relaxing way.

☺ Now, close your eyes and listen to the sounds around you. How many different sounds can you count?

☺ Take 30 more seconds. Sit quietly while you look and feel everything around you. Keep breathing calmly and slowly, in and out.

What do you notice?

How do you feel now? How is it different from how you felt one minute ago?

What do you notice? In the present moment, everything is fine, right?

FUN FACT: Taking deep, calming breaths when you are feeling anxious actually helps your body to bypass your "fight or flight" response, which helps allow you to respond rationally to the situation at hand. When people are tense, their natural reaction is to take short, shallow breaths. These breaths do not get the necessary oxygen into their lungs. Instead, shallow breathing causes a buildup of CO_2 in the bloodstream, and has the opposite effect. It makes you feel more tense and worried!

Any time you are nervous, pause and breathe slowly. Your relaxed response will confuse the Worry Monster and scare that trouble-maker away! Practice your belly breathing with slow, deep breaths—just like you were doing in the *Staying in the Present* exercise. Make a plan to practice this at least a few times a day.

Activity:

Think about or reflect on *Staying in the Present.*

What are some reasons for staying in the present moment instead of worrying about the past?

_____

What are some reasons for staying in the present moment instead of worrying about the *future*?

_____

It is normal to sometimes feel upset or concerned about something that seems scary. You may think about everything bad that might happen in the future, or feel guilty about things that have happened in the past. If you stay in the present, though, it is easier to deal with these feelings without becoming overwhelmed. You can't undo the past, and you can't control the future. All you can manage is you—right now in the present.

What are some of the things you can do with worries you have that can't be changed right away? Here is an example of a toolbox for your worries...

"Plan for what to do if it does happen."
~ Scarlett

"Always focus on the positive, not the negative."
~ Grayson

☺ Practice letting Worry Monster thoughts pass. Don't obsess over them; just notice and acknowledge them, saying, "Hmmmm, it's interesting that I am thinking that thought. I'll deal with you when the time is right."

☺ Use positive self-talk. Tell yourself, "I can do this!"

☺ Talk back to the Worry Monster. Tell that pest to "Beat it! I'm busy."

☺ Distract yourself with another activity, especially one that requires a high level of focus.

☺ Seek support from a friend, parent, or teacher.

☺ Reserve your worries for worry time later. Put your worries in a jar in your mind, and screw the lid on tight. Then give yourself _____ minutes. You can open the jar later.

☺ Take deep breaths.

☺ Ask yourself what you are thinking and write it down.

☺ Tell your amygdala to stop going wild! Especially if the thought is irrational.

☺ Close your eyes and count to ten.

☺ Draw a picture of how you feel.

☺ Write a list of your worries to use for writing funny stories later.

☺ Repeat a positive mantra. (i.e. "All is well. I am safe.")

☺ Lie on your back with your favorite stuffed animal. Inhale through your nose and count to three. Exhale through your mouth and count to three. Watch your stuffed animal buddy rise and fall as you breathe. Repeat this until you feel better.

Do you have your own ideas? Add them to the list.

1. _____

2. _____

3. _____

4. _____

5. _____

CHAPTER 8

Behavioral Interventions: Practice, Practice, Practice!

"Act the way you want to feel."

~ Gretchen Rubin

"A ship in harbor is safe,
but that is not what ships were built for."

~ John Shedd

Athletes, students, and musicians all use practice to build skills. You may practice the balance beam, free throws, tennis or golf, spelling, driving, or any number of other things.

Why do we practice? We practice to get better at something, so that it comes more naturally to us. Eventually, some of our skills can even become automatic. So, how about practicing doing the things we are afraid of? Whoa! That's kind of a scary thought, isn't it? Let's say that another way: how about practicing doing the things that will defeat the Worry Monster who is trying to trick us and control our lives?

Practice is key to working through our fears. It is essential to practice behaviors that allow us to let go of our fears. This way we can conquer the fears that are holding us back, keeping us from feeling good, taking chances, and meeting our full potential.

Important Word #4

Exposure: The act of uncovering or revealing a new experience or experiencing something.

"Getting over a painful experience is much like crossing monkey bars. You have to let go at some point in order to move forward."

~C.S. Lewis

Exposure gives you the opportunity to break down a big goal into small, manageable steps. As you move forward, one step at a time, you can become familiar with your fear. Eventually, you may even become bored with it! With practice, and over time, each step in the process becomes easier. Eventually, you reach the top—conquering the fear completely!

One student called these steps "The steps to a good life!" Think of a big goal for yourself. What fears hold you back from that?

Write your big goal here: _____

_____

Can you think of fears that hold you back from reaching that goal? Write them here:

_____

_____

Fill the brainstorm cloud below with ideas for ways that you can gradually "expose" yourself to your fear—one small step at a time. Include any ideas you have including: not scary/easy for you to do, kind of scary/moderate, and very scary/hard to do. Remember, this can include things that you WILL do, and also things that you will NOT do. Sometimes it can be scary to even think about these things. As you do, remember to stay in the moment. Take deep belly breaths if you need to!

Success Ladder

A success ladder is something that will help you to overcome your fears one step at a time. A success ladder is a ladder that starts with the easiest step toward overcoming your fear and works up to the harder ones. For example, if you are afraid of dogs, your easiest step might be to look at a book about dogs. A more moderate step might be to pet a dog that is on a leash. A hard step might be to go to a friend's house or park where a dog is off leash. Try using the ideas from your exposure brainstorm cloud to fill in a success ladder for yourself.

Hardest Step

10	
9	
8	
7	
6	
5	
4	
3	
2	
1	

Easiest Step

As you move along your success ladder, you will want to be well prepared with things you can do to keep the Worry Monster away, or to tame the scoundrel if it shows up. Making a plan and being prepared will help you be more successful! Exposing yourself to your worries may feel uncomfortable at first, and you may feel like you want to respond the way you always have. Fight that urge! This is a great time to start climbing the ladder to positive change, even if at first you have to "fake it until you make it."

As you go up each step in your success ladder, visualize what victory will look like. At first, you may not feel like a winner, even though you were able to expose yourself to some of what you were worried about. But if you act like a winner, you are more likely to become a winner. Try smiling and putting on a brave face when you feel worried. Or try replacing negative thoughts with positive ones. Make a list of ways that you can feel like a winner as you make your journey up the success ladder.

1. _____

2. _____

3. _____

4. _____

5. _____

Having a plan of action in place can help you with your worries and fears. Just knowing what you would do if the worry actually were to occur can be helpful. For example, if your fear is that you might be left at school, and one day you actually WERE left at school, what information would you need? What would you do? You would need to know where to find the school office, and you would need to know your parents' phone numbers. With this information ready, you would be able to have the office call your parents. You might even want to have extra information (such as the number of a family friend) so that you have a backup. As one person said, "Knowledge is power." This will give you power over the Worry Monster. By thinking things through ahead of time, you expose yourself to your worry, making it less scary.

> "It's kind of helpful, because now you know what would happen in that situation."
> ~ Scarlett

List what you will need to do in the event your big worry actually did come true. What would you need?

Information I will need:

_____

_____

What I will do:

_____

_____

Things I will need:

_____

_____

Important Word #5

Resilience: Being able to recover quickly from diffulties.

"Do not judge me by my successes. Judge me by
how many times I fell down and got back up again."
~ Nelson Mandela

"It's fine to celebrate success but it is
more important to heed the lessons of failure."
~ Bill Gates

"Develop success from failures. Discouragement and
failure are two of the surest steppingstones to success."
~ Dale Carnegie

Being resilient means being able to handle problems that come your way. It means coping with them, and finding solutions to them.

Things may not turn out the way you expect them to, and that is okay. The most brilliant artists, thinkers, inventors, entrepreneurs, and other Worriers-turned-Warriors of the world all found their success through trial and error. They weren't ever perfect, but instead worked hard, conquered their fears, and learned a lot along the way.

What can you do if your plan does not turn out the way you expect it to? What worrisome thoughts might you have if you aren't perfectly able to reach your goal, and what positive thoughts can you replace them with? Lastly, think about all the work you put in to try and reach your goal, regardless of whether or not you succeeded. How did you do—OVERALL? It may have gone well. Even if you didn't reach your ultimate goal, you have victories to celebrate. Remember: every step is progress, and success comes in many forms. Take your last project. What successes can you count? Well, first of all, you took a risk. Second, you made the effort. Third, you made some progress in fighting off the Worry Monster. What other victories associated with this goal can you celebrate?

Here are some examples of successes from the kids in our class! Each of them describes a time when working through their worry led to everything turning out fine!

"Dad was gone for a week, and I was worried. When he came back, he was fine."

~ *Cole*

"I went on an elevator and it had a TV! That was cool!"

~*Scarlett*

I went on the Tower of Terror ride, and it was fine. It was short!"

~ *Myles*

"When I moved, I was afraid the kids there wouldn't like me and they wouldn't be my friend. But it turned out fine!"

~ *Grayson*

Important Word #6

Perfectionism: Where failure to be perfect is unacceptable and makes you feel worthless.

"I am learning that perfection isn't what matters.
In fact, it's the very thing that can destroy you if you let it."
~ Emily Giffin

"Perfectionism doesn't believe in practice shots.
It doesn't believe in improvement. Perfectionism has
never heard that anything worth doing is worth doing
badly—and that if we allow ourselves to do something
badly we might in time become quite good at it."
~ Julia Cameron

Perfectionism often produces an intense fear that can stop you in your tracks. You can feel so paralyzed by perfectionism that you can't even get started. Fear of starting can cause you to procrastinate. It can make you feel worried, uptight, and bothered by the idea that nothing you do will ever be good enough.

Of course, it is good to set high goals for yourself, but no one is perfect all of the time. In fact, most people spend a long time being imperfect at something before they even become good at it. In order to become your best, it is important that you cut yourself a break. You need to embrace the idea that nobody is perfect.

Sometimes, kids struggling with perfectionism get so worried about doing everything just right that they either won't start an activity, or they will take longer than they need to in order to complete it. This can make life difficult!

Dealing with perfectionism often requires a plan.

Is there something that you have had trouble doing because you have been afraid it won't be perfect? Write it down here.

_____

_____

_____

Do you sometimes feel things **have** to be done perfectly? Does this make these things harder to complete? What can you do to avoid this unrealistic level of expectation? Are there some things that you can do that don't need to be perfect? Are you able to accept *good enough*? (This is called "planned imperfection," and describes moments where you consciously plan not to be perfect.)

For example, if you were given an assignment, what might you do to ensure you do it well, but that you don't worry about perfection? Perhaps you might think of what would be good enough rather than perfect.

Try your hand at planned imperfection here. Think of a task you might have (such as a school assignment) and list some ideas about how to do it **well**, but not perfect. Remember, if you need help, you can always ask a trusted adult.

1. _____

2. _____

3. _____

Who can you check with to make sure your plan for imperfection is a good one? What are the steps and timeline for completing the key parts of your activity?

1. _____

2. _____

3. _____

4. _____

5. _____

6. _____

If the assignment is something you are avoiding, you may want to commit to spending a little more time on it. If it is something that might take longer than you think it should, then you will want to set a time boundary for yourself. For example, "I will try a new song and practice piano for twenty minutes each day." Or, "I know that this assignment should only take me twenty minutes, and so I am going to outline what should be done at 5, 10, and 15 minutes to keep me on track with my goal."

Use the worksheet on the next page to help you plan. Planning ahead is one surefire way to ensure success! It may take a bit of time to learn at first, but soon you'll be able to make plans and prepare yourself quickly!

What new thoughts can you use to combat your Worry Monster thoughts?

Worry Monster Thought	My New Thought
"If I don't do the whole thing perfectly, I will look bad to everyone."	"Some parts of the project will be better than others, and that's okay."

Perfectionism Worksheet

My Goal: _____

What are some things I can do to make sure that I meet (but not exceed) the expectations that I set for myself?

_____

_____

Do I have part-way goals along the way? How will I can accomplish my part-way goals and my final goal? How will I know when I've met them?

_____

_____

What things can I let go, or relax about a little bit, in order to focus on achieving my goal? (Like, *planned imperfection* or *doing good enough*).

_____

_____

Manageable Steps for Achieving My Goal:

_____

_____

Worry Worksheet

Write down your worry here:

_____

_____

What is making you feel like this worry might come true? What evidence do you have that it might come true?

_____

_____

What steps can you take today to help you overcome this worry?

_____

_____

What information will you need in order to take these steps?

_____

_____

What can you expect to feel as you work through your worry?

_____

_____

Your Toolbox

What are you going to carry in your "toolbox" to help you feel more prepared for the Worry Monster if he decides to show up? You can use the tools from Dr. Dan's Toolbox below, and you can add your own!

☺ Take deep breaths.

☺ Focus on the present moment.

☺ Use positive self-talk ("I can do this!").

☺ Ask yourself what you are thinking.

☺ Change your thinking.

☺ Talk back to the Worry Monster ("Take a hike, you cowardly bully!").

☺ Ignore the Worry Monster ("So what?").

☺ Distract yourself with another activity.

☺ Exercise.

☺ Seek support from a friend, parent, or teacher.

☺ Use your worry box.

☺ Reserve your worries for worry time later.

_____

Make a prediction: When you take this step toward overcoming your worry, how awful do you think it is going to be? Circle your rating here:

Awful   1   2   3   4   5   6   7   8   9   10   Great

How will you know you are making progress overcoming this worry? What positive changes will you see?

_____

Reflecting Upon Your Victory!

Even if things didn't go perfectly, you should feel proud of yourself and celebrate. Steps toward overcoming your worry—even small ones—are victories!

Go back to your prediction. Was taking this step toward overcoming your worry really as awful as you expected? Circle   Yes   or   No

Rate how difficult it was below:

Awful   1   2   3   4   5   6   7   8   9   10   Great

What was difficult for you? What challenges did you have to overcome in order to achieve your goal?

_____

What went well?

_____

What didn't go as well as you hoped?

_____

Did you learn anything new that will help you with your next success ladder?

_____

How are you going to celebrate your victory!?

_____

If you'd like to chart your progress moving up the success ladder, head to the end of the book. We've made a handy "star chart" just for you.

Important Word #7

Perspective: How we choose to see the world.

"Change the way you look at things
and the things you look at change."
~ Wayne W. Dyer

"To change ourselves effectively,
we first had to change our perceptions."
~ Stephen R. Covey

An Up Side to Worry?

When worry controls our ability to fully participate in or enjoy life, it is never a good thing. But hopefully, by facing your worries, you have come to realize that you are brave and strong. You can overcome things that are difficult for you, even when they sometimes feel impossible.

Worry often stems from very strong feelings about things that are important to you and that you care about very much, and it is good to have things that are important to you.

It may be important to you to be the best you can be for the people you care about, or you may care so much about someone, like a parent, that you never want to be away from them. Caring this much is a very special and good thing, but this type of caring can lead to worry and fear.

So, when you feel worry creeping in, you might say to yourself, "Thanks for this worry feeling, Worry Monster. It reminds me that I have things I care about very much. Now go away!"

It's okay to thank the Worry Monster. After all, he has taught you some important lessons. Make a list on the next page of the special people, places, and things in your life. List the things that you care about and are grateful for. And remember: being free from the Worry Monster allows you to be your best for all the people and things on your list. That's good for everyone.

FUN FACT: Gratitude is directly linked to the pleasure centers of your brain. When these areas of the brain are stimulated, your body produces chemicals that make you feel confident, connected, and, well, just good!

My Gratitude List

Here is a list of people, places and things that are special to me that I am happy to have in my life, and that make me feel content, safe, and appreciated.

Special People

_____

_____

_____

_____

Special Places and Things

_____

_____

_____

_____

Take Advantage of Your Worry!

By now, you've learned about the different ways your body can react to fear and worry. Remember the 3000-pound car? When you start to feel a worry coming on, remember what you have learned. Remember that you are strong!

Once you have become comfortable challenging the Worry Monster, you won't have to worry so much. You may even welcome the feelings the worry Monster brings; you may see them as challenges you know you can learn to overcome. When you've beaten the Worry Monster, the challenges and fears that used to made you feel anxious might even start to seem like fun!

"Everything is created twice,
first in the mind and then in reality."
~Robin S. Sharma

"That the birds of worry and care fly over your head,
this you cannot change, but that they build nests
in your hair, this you can prevent."
~ Chinese Proverb

"Somehow our devils are never quite what
we expect when we meet them face to face."
~ Nelson DeMille

You are a Warrior!

You now know more about the brain, our body's survival system, worry, anxiety, and coping skills than many adults in the world! You are armed with knowledge, and knowledge is power! You have the power to understand how the Worry Monster bullies you into feeling scared, worried, and weak. You also have the power to fight back by ignoring him, using his strategies against him, and making him scared of you because you are the one with the power, not him. You have SO many tools to defeat him and to be in charge of your life!

Remember to share your victories with your friends and family members. Not only will it make your victories stronger and the worry monster weaker, it will also help your friends and family members to fight their own Worry Monster. Never forget that you are strong and awesome!

Look at the poor weak Worry Monster shrinking. Bye bye, Worry Monster. We won't miss you.

...poof!

A Letter to the Worry Monster

Now that you have come so far in your journey from Worrier to Warrior, it's time to write a letter to the Worry Monster. Let that mischief-maker know that it is no longer welcome in your life. Yes, you may have become used to having it around in the past, and the Worry Monster even pretended to let you feel safe for a while, but now you know better. Tell that trouble-maker about the feelings and ways of thinking that you won't tolerate anymore, and all the good things you experience now that you are becoming free. Make sure the Worry Monster knows what to expect if it tries to sneak up and scare you again. The Worry Monster may continue to try, but you are ready for it. From now on, you're ready to conquer your fears, and to be a real Warrior!

Dear Worry Monster,

_____

_____

_____

_____

_____

_____

Signed,

Appendices

Star Chart!!!

A Record of Your Success

As you work through your worries, be sure to record your victories!

1. List your worry.

2. List the step you took toward overcoming your worry.

3. List the outcome.

4. Give yourself a star!

5. Be sure to look back at your great progress over time.

Worried Thought	Success Ladder Step	New Thought	Outcome	Place your star below!

My Daily Journal

Three good things that happened today are:

1. _____

2. _____

3. _____

I am grateful for:

_____

_____

I am looking forward to:

_____

_____

What's on my mind...

_____

_____

"Don't be afraid of your fears. They're not there to scare you.
They're there to let you know that something is worth it."
~ C. JoyBell C.

Worry Tickets

Here are some Worry Tickets. Please copy this page so you can cut out the Worry Tickets to use for each worry. By making a copy of this page, you can keep your Workbook intact

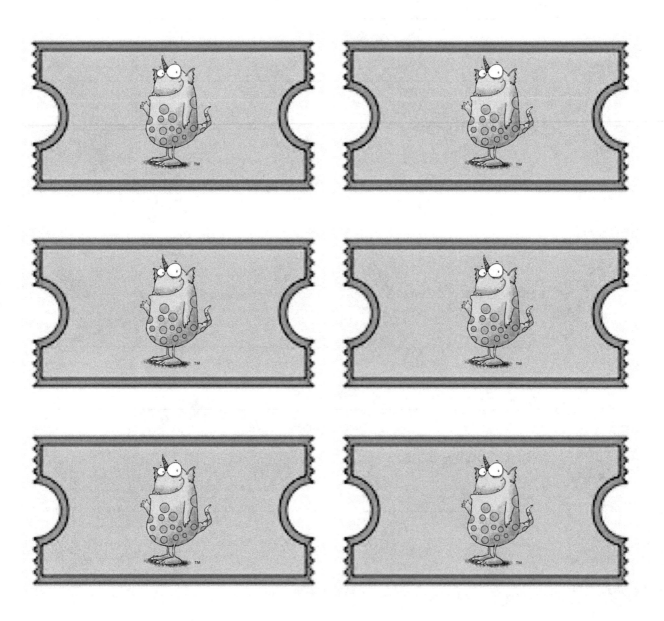

Worry Monster Crossword Challenge!

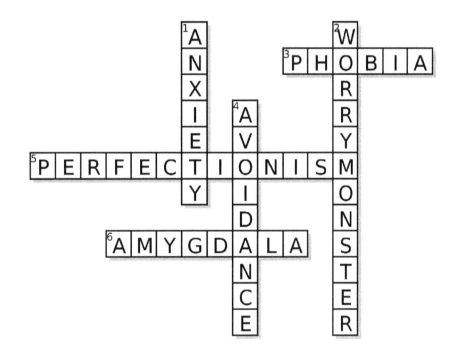

About the Authors

Dr. Dan Peters is a psychologist, author, co-founder, and Executive Director of the Summit Center. Dr. Peters has devoted his career to the assessment and treatment of children, adolescents, and families, specializing in overcoming worry and fear, learning differences such as dyslexia, and issues related to giftedness and twice-exceptionality.

Dr. Dan is also co-founder of Parent Footprint, an interactive parenting education community and website that offers Parent Footprint Awareness Training with the mission to make the world a more compassionate and loving place—one parent and one child at a time. He is host of the "Parent Footprint Podcast with Dr. Dan" and is a regular contributor to *The Huffington Post* and *Psychology Today*.

For over 20 years, Dr. Dan has been passionate about helping parents to guide their children with purpose and intention to help them in reaching their potential while their children are also reaching their own. Dr. Dan is the author of *Make Your Worrier a Warrior: A Guide to Conquering Your Child's Fears* (Great Potential Press, 2013) and its companion children's book *From Worrier to Warrior*, is a contributor to the new book *toughLOVE: Raising Confident, Kind, Resilient Kids* and co-author of *Raising Creative Kids* as well as many articles on topics related to parenting, family, giftedness, twice-exceptionality, dyslexia, and anxiety.

Dr. Dan speaks frequently at national conferences and to the media on a variety of topics including parenting, learning differences, special needs, family, education and more. He serves on the California Association for the Gifted (CAG) Advisory Board, the Supporting Emotional Needs of Gifted (SENG) Editorial Board, the Editorial Board for the 2e Newsletter, the Advisory Board for the 2e Center for Research and Professional Development at Bridges Academy, and as Co-Chair of the Assessments of Giftedness Special Interest Group of the National Association of Gifted

Children (NAGC). He is also co-founder of Camp Summit, a sleep-over summer camp for gifted youth.

Dr. Lisa Reid has served as a teacher and an administrator in the K-12 teaching system for over a decade. She specializes in working with children who have complex learning needs such as dyslexia, ADHD, poor motivation, sensory processing issues, low academic self-esteem, performance anxiety, and poor social and executive functioning skills. Dr. Reid has been particularly dedicated to making a difference in the lives of children who display learning related behavioral challenges, children who display higher level thinking ability yet underachieve, and children who are gifted but often find themselves in trouble or misunderstood due to their intense nature, social/emotional challenges, and/or learning difficulties. She is dedicated to recognizing the inner integrity of all children, and helping them to reach their full potential as learners. Dr. Reid provides parent support, group instruction, private educational therapy, educational consultation, and teacher trainings in Orange County, CA.

Reid holds a Doctorate in Education in Curriculum and Instruction with a secondary emphasis in Educational Psychology, a Masters in Education in Curriculum and Instruction with a secondary emphasis in Gifted Education and a Bachelors in Biology. Additionally, Reid is a SENG Model Parent Group Facilitator, an Educational Therapist/Professional (ET/P) with the Association of Educational Therapists, holds a California State Teaching Certification and is a Certified "Critical Friends Group" Counselor. She has won numerous awards including a 2015 Nomination for the SENG Honor Roll of Outstanding Educators, a 2009 Rancho Solano Private School Excellence in Education Award, a 2008 Xavier College Preparatory Golden Gator Award for Excellence in Teaching, and a 2008 Meritas Lead Teacher honor.

Stephanie Davis. M.Ed., is a teacher and Educational Therapist, with extensive training in learning disabilities and intervention strategies specific to learning differences. Her education includes a Master in Education and teaching credential from University of California Los Angeles, and the Educational Therapy Certification from University of California Riverside. She interned at Kaiser Watts Counseling and Learning Center, where she furthered her skills in assessment and intervention. She is dedicated to addressing the comprehensive needs of a child: academic, non-academic, and social-emotional. A very special culture is created within her private sessions and within her current role as Resource Specialist. Stephanie strives to make an astonishing difference in the lives of her students, as they strive to become their ideal selves. She lives in Southern California with her three children, two cats and a puppy.

CPSIA information can be obtained
at www.ICGtesting.com
Printed in the USA
LVHW011649070521
686745LV00004B/47